P9-BAU-045

DATE DUE

DISCARD

PLEASE WASH
YOUR HANDS
BEFORE YOU READ ME
AND KEEP ME CLEAN

HOSPITAL WORKERS
in the
Emergency Room

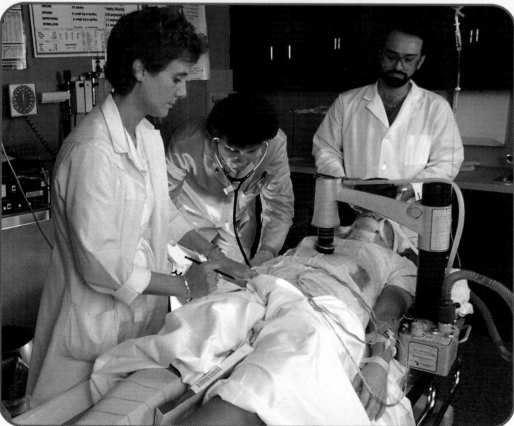

Bobbie Kalman

❦ Crabtree Publishing Company

www.crabtreebooks.com

Created by Bobbie Kalman

Dedicated by Tara Arlant
For my beautiful sons, Evan and Avery, who I love so much!

Author and Editor-in-Chief
Bobbie Kalman

Substantive editor
Kathryn Smithyman

Project editor and research
Reagan Miller

Editors
Molly Aloian
Kristina Lundblad
Kelley MacAulay

Art director
Robert MacGregor

Design
Margaret Amy Reiach
Samantha Crabtree (series logo)

Production coordinator
Katherine Kantor

Photo research
Crystal Foxton

Consultant
Dr. Tony Woodward, Chief of Emergency Services,
Children's Hospital and Regional Medical Center,
Seattle, Washington

Special thanks
Sandra Tkach

Photographs
Marc Crabtree: page 31
Copyright DoctorStock.com: pages 13, 30
Jupiter Images: pages 5, 18
Antonia Reeve/Photo Researchers, Inc.: page 21
Other images by Brand X Pictures, Corbis,
Digital Stock, and Photodisc

Illustrations
Margaret Amy Reiach: border
Bonna Rouse: pages 14, 15, 16, 29, 31

Crabtree Publishing Company

www.crabtreebooks.com   1-800-387-7650

Copyright © **2005 CRABTREE PUBLISHING COMPANY.**
All rights reserved. No part of this publication may be
reproduced, stored in a retrieval system or be transmitted in
any form or by any means, electronic, mechanical, photocopying,
recording, or otherwise, without the prior written permission
of Crabtree Publishing Company. In Canada: We acknowledge the
financial support of the Government of Canada through the Book
Publishing Industry Development Program (BPIDP) for our
publishing activities.

Cataloging-in-Publication Data
Kalman, Bobbie.
  Hospital workers in the emergency room / Bobbie Kalman.
    p. cm. -- (My community and its helpers series)
  Includes index.
  ISBN 0-7787-2095-0 (RLB) -- ISBN 0-7787-2123-X (pbk.)
  1. Hospitals--Emergency service--Juvenile literature. 2
Hospitals--Staff--Juvenile literature. I. Title.
  RA975.5.E5K356 2005
  362.18'0683--dc22
                                                    2004014179
                                                    LC

**Published in
the United States**
PMB16A
350 Fifth Ave.
Suite 3308
New York, NY
10118

**Published
in Canada**
616 Welland Ave.,
St. Catharines, Ontario,
Canada
L2M 5V6

**Published in the
United Kingdom**
73 Lime Walk
Headington
Oxford
OX3 7AD
United Kingdom

**Published
in Australia**
386 Mt. Alexander Rd.,
Ascot Vale (Melbourne)
VIC 3032

Contents

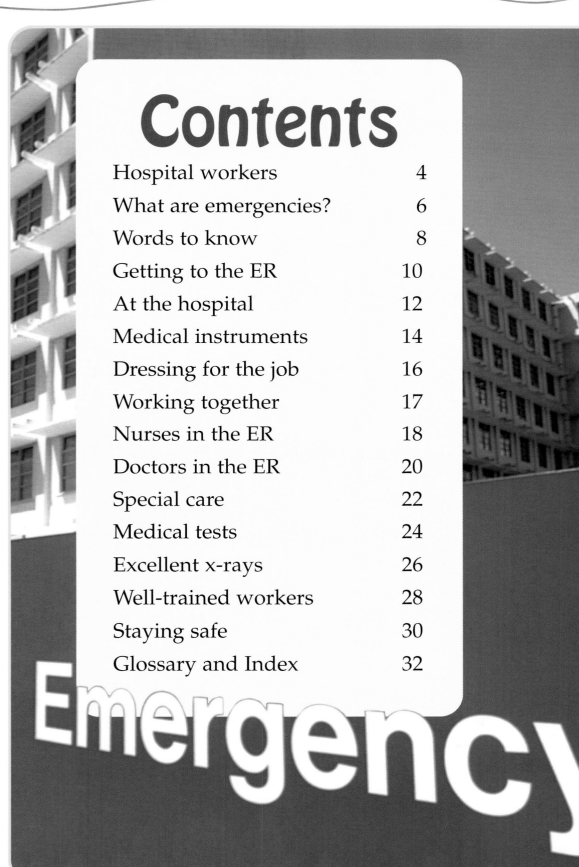

Emergency

Hospital workers

Hospital workers are people who work in hospitals. This book is about hospital workers who work in the **emergency room** or "ER." The ER is the area in a hospital where people go when they need medical help right away. The ER is also called the **emergency department**. Doctors, nurses, and other hospital workers in the ER give medical care to people who are sick or hurt.

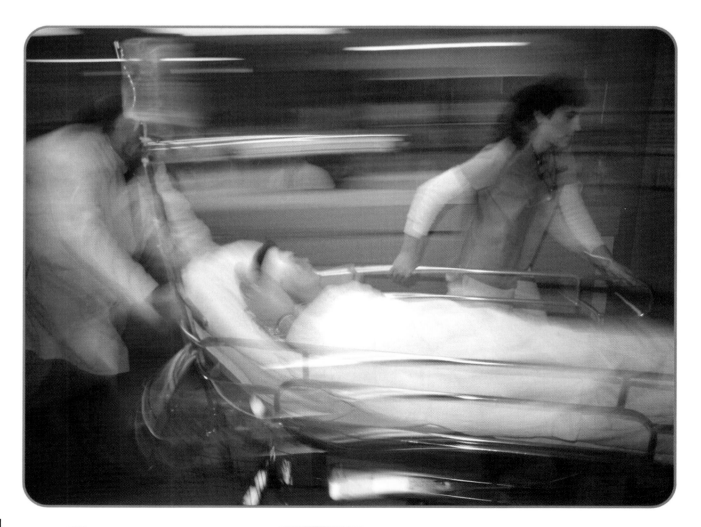

Who are community helpers?

Hospital workers are **community helpers**. A **community** is an area and the people who live in that area. Community helpers are people who help keep communities safe and healthy. Hospital workers are important community helpers because they know how to care for people who are sick or hurt. Police officers, firefighters, veterinarians, dentists, and construction workers are other community helpers.

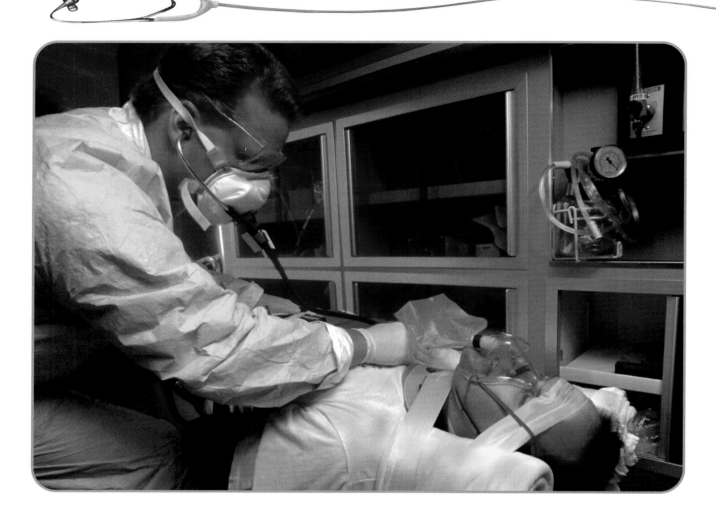

What are emergencies?

Emergencies are serious situations that may threaten people's lives. Emergencies can happen at any time, and they often happen without any warning. Some emergencies are **medical emergencies**, such as serious illnesses or **injuries**. An injury is harm caused to a person's body. Some injuries are caused when people hurt other people. Other injuries are caused by accidents such as fires, falling from high places, swimming and boating accidents, or car wrecks. People must act quickly to help others during medical emergencies.

Emergency illnesses

Sudden illnesses can be emergencies. When a person has a very high **fever** or has trouble breathing, he or she needs to get to the emergency room quickly! That person could have a serious disease, such as **meningitis** or **pneumonia**. Pneumonia is a disease that affects a person's **lungs**.

Contagious diseases

Some diseases are **contagious**. Contagious diseases spread easily from one person to another. Some, such as **Severe Acute Respiratory Syndrome** or "SARS," can even spread around the world! When hospital workers suspect that a patient has a contagious disease, they must be very careful!

Fast action

ER nurses and doctors act quickly when they believe a sick person may have a contagious disease that can cause death. They move the sick person to an area of the hospital that is away from other people so the disease does not spread. All hospital workers know to take special care when they are near a person who has a contagious disease. They put on special clothing before they help the sick person.

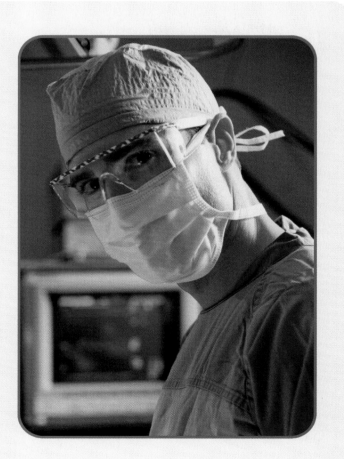

Words to know

The words on these pages are used often in this book. Knowing what they mean will help you understand the information you are reading. To learn more medical words, turn to page 32.

treat To give medical care

treatment The care that is given for an illness or injury

To treat this girl's broken legs, the doctor is putting casts on them. This treatment will help her legs heal.

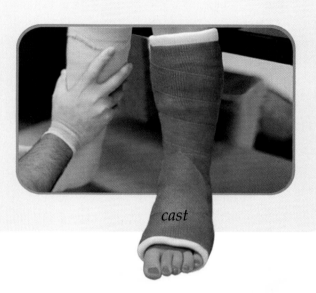

cast

examine To look closely and carefully at someone to see what might be wrong

A doctor examines this girl's throat to find out why it hurts.

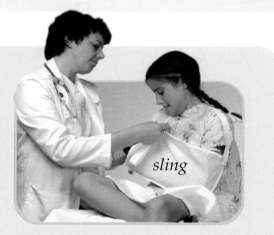

sling

patient A person who is being given medical care or who is in a hospital

The doctor is putting a sling on her patient's injured arm.

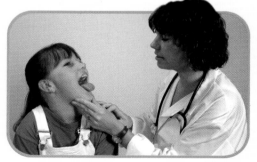

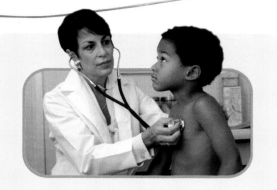

diagnose To identify a patient's illness or injury by examining him or her

Listening to the child's heart will help the doctor diagnose the child's illness.

admit To ask a patient to stay in the hospital so he or she can receive extra medical care

A doctor admitted this boy because his injuries were serious.

prescription A written order for medicine

prescribe To order a treatment or a type of medicine

Doctors write prescriptions for medicines. They may prescribe plenty of rest as well as medicine.

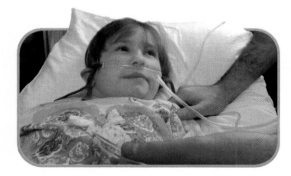

stabilize To care for a patient so that his or her illness or injury does not get worse

*Hospital workers have stabilized this girl by giving her **oxygen**.*

Getting to the ER

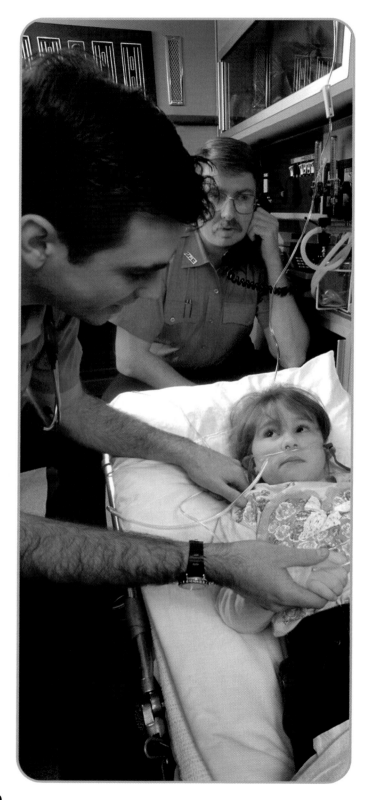

In an emergency, people need to get to a hospital quickly. The fastest and safest way to get someone to a hospital is in an ambulance. **Emergency medical service**, or "EMS" workers drive ambulances to emergencies to pick up people and take them to hospitals. EMS workers also give people **first aid**, or basic medical care.

Paramedics

Paramedics are EMS workers that are trained to give people medicine. They are also trained to use machines that give electric shocks to patients' hearts. Shocking a heart helps it beat normally.

These EMS workers are on their way to a hospital with a young patient.

Bright lights and sirens

Ambulances have bright flashing lights and loud sirens. The lights and sirens warn other cars on the road to move out of the way! Ambulances need to get through traffic so they can reach hospitals safely and quickly.

Medical care on the move

Ambulances are stocked with medical supplies such as bandages and medicines. EMS workers use these supplies to care for people during the ambulance ride to the hospital. Their most important job is to stabilize patients while they are traveling to a hospital.

Radio ahead

EMS workers use radios to contact hospital workers in the emergency room. They give the doctors in the ER information about the patients they are treating in the ambulance.

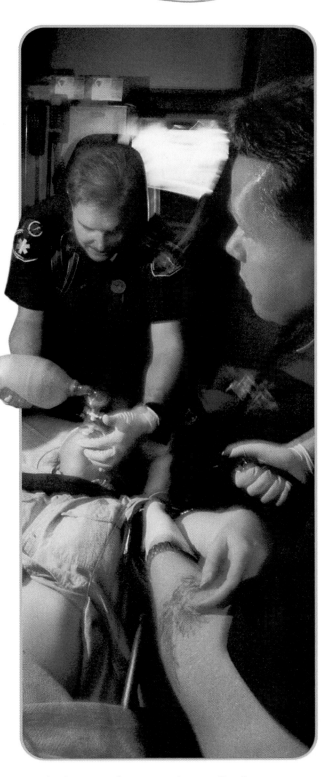

*Ambulances also contain medical equipment such as **air bags**. An EMS worker is using an air bag to pump oxygen into a patient's lungs. The oxygen helps the patient breathe more easily.*

At the hospital

The hospital workers in the ER are prepared for almost any type of emergency. When they receive radio messages from EMS workers, they start getting supplies and equipment ready. Doctors and nurses sometimes rush outside to meet the ambulance when it arrives! The **ambulance bay** is located near the ER. The ambulance bay is a special driveway where ambulances can stop safely. Large doors between the ER and the ambulance bay slide open to allow people to move **gurneys** through the doors in a hurry. A gurney is a bed on wheels, which is used to move a patient.

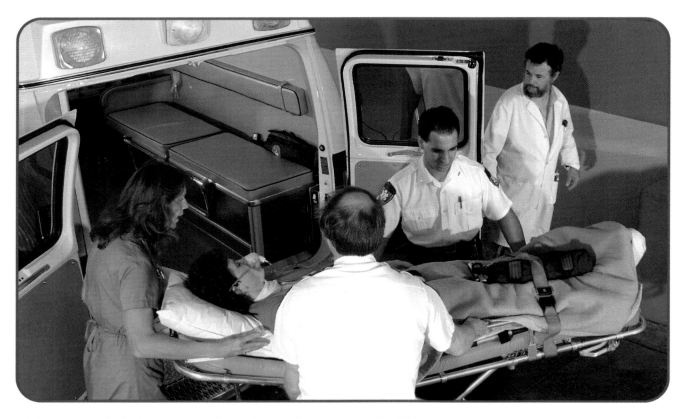

This patient is being moved from the ambulance to the ER on a gurney.

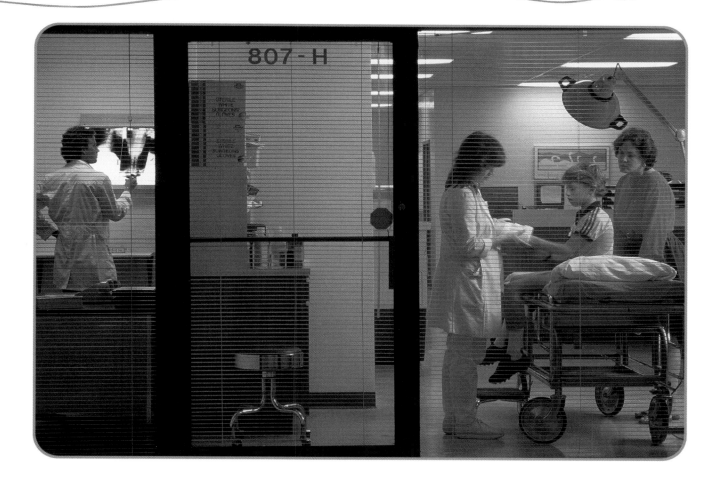

Arriving at the ER

People who arrive at the ER have different kinds of illnesses or injuries. It is important that the patients with the most serious illnesses or injuries are the first to see the doctors. As people arrive, **triage nurses** quickly examine them and ask them questions. The triage nurses then decide who needs help right away.

Treatment rooms

Patients who need immediate help are taken to **treatment rooms**. In these rooms, doctors and nurses examine the patients and treat them. People with injuries or illnesses that are not life-threatening may have to wait before they can see a doctor. People who are waiting to see a doctor sit in the **waiting room**.

Medical instruments

Doctors and nurses use special **instruments,** or tools, to examine their patients. The instruments may look strange and scary, but they help doctors and nurses find out what is wrong with their patients. If you are ever in an emergency room, you may see some of the medical tools shown on these pages.

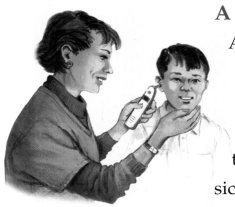

A thermometer

A hospital worker takes your temperature by placing a **thermometer** in your mouth or in your ear. A thermometer measures the temperature of your body. When you are healthy, your body temperature is about 98.6°F (37°C). When you are sick, your body temperature may rise. If your body temperature rises higher than normal, you have a fever.

A stethoscope

A doctor or a nurse may use a **stethoscope** to listen to your heartbeat. A stethoscope is also used to listen to your lungs as you breathe. Your lungs are inside your chest. They take in and let out air.

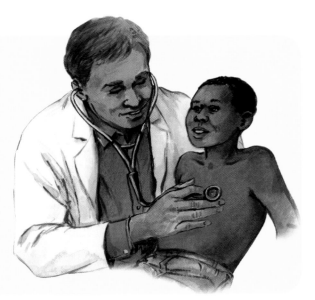

A blood-pressure cuff

A **blood-pressure cuff** measures how hard your heart is working. To take your blood pressure, a hospital worker wraps the cuff around your arm and pumps it full of air. You will feel a squeeze as the cuff tightens around your arm. The hospital worker then puts a stethoscope on your arm to listen as your heart pumps blood through the arm.

An IV

An **intravenous** (IV) is a tiny tube with a needle at one end. The needle is used to push the tube gently into a **vein** in your arm. The tube is attached to a bag that contains medicine. The medicine drips through the tube into your vein.

An otoscope

An **otoscope** is a medical instrument with a light at its end. The light helps a doctor look inside your nose and ears to see if anything is wrong with them.

Dressing for the job

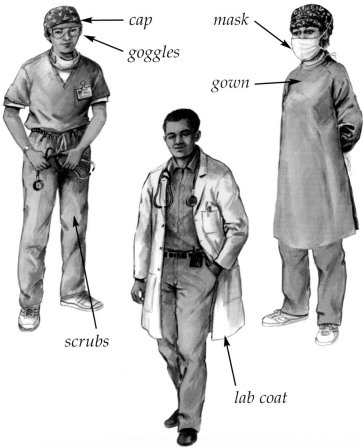

cap

goggles

mask

gown

scrubs

lab coat

Doctors, nurses, and other hospital workers wear different kinds of clothing in the ER. Doctors often wear their own clothing when they visit patients. They protect their clothes by wearing white coats called **lab coats**. In the ER and in surgery, doctors wear **scrubs**. Scrubs are loose-fitting, comfortable clothing. Many other hospital workers also wear scrubs.

Extra protection

Hospital workers can spread germs from one patient to another if they wear the same clothes when they visit several sick patients. To stop germs from spreading, doctors and nurses often wear **disposable clothing**.

Disposable clothing is worn once and is then thrown away. Disposable items such as gloves, caps, masks, and gowns help protect patients. They also protect hospital workers from catching the diseases of their patients.

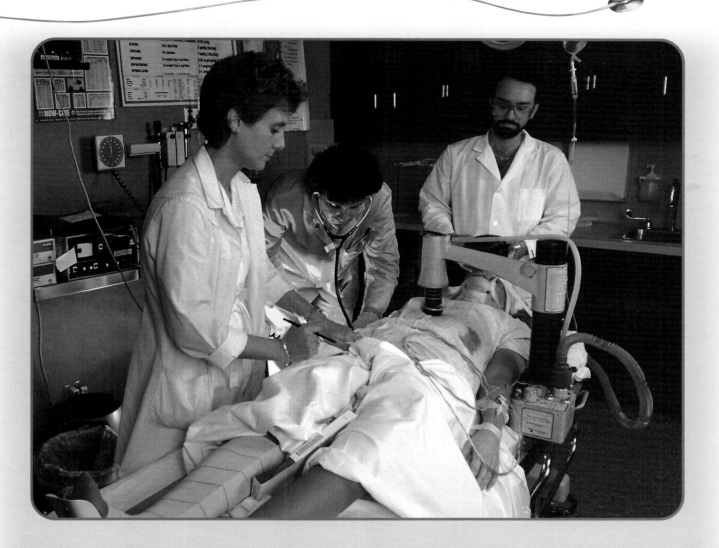

Working together

Each hospital worker is trained to do
a specific job. In emergencies, however,
doctors, nurses, and other hospital workers
work as a team. They work quickly to make
sure that patients receive the best medical
help they can get. Hospital workers know
that by working together, they can care for
many patients at the same time.

Nurses in the ER

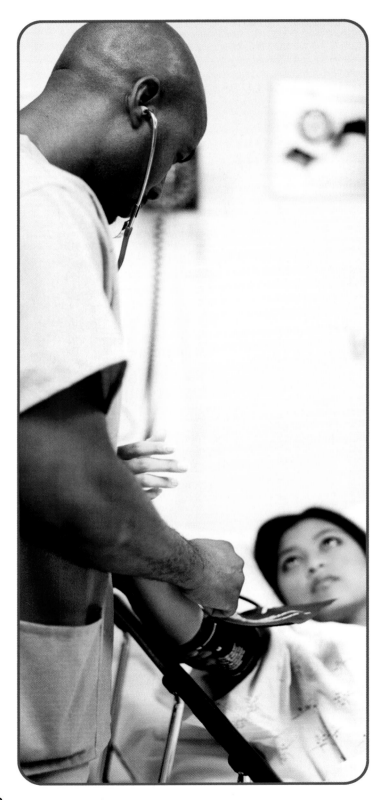

Without nurses, patients in the ER would not receive proper care! Nurses do many jobs. They know how to care for patients with different illnesses and injuries. Each nurse in the ER cares for several patients. Nurses keep track of what each patient needs.

Caring for patients

Nurses work closely with doctors. They clean and bandage cuts and scrapes. They give sick or injured patients medicines that have been prescribed by doctors. Nurses also check on patients several times each hour. They take each patient's temperature and blood pressure. Nurses are a great help to their patients.

Care and comfort

Some of the patients who come to the ER are confused and frightened. The nurses in the ER comfort them. They talk with the patients and answer their questions so they will not be afraid. They also talk with the families of the patients. Nurses explain the treatments the patients are receiving.

Important information

Nurses keep a **chart** for every patient in the emergency room. The chart contains medical information about the patient. For example, a nurse asks a patient if he or she is **allergic** to any kind of medicine and writes that information on the chart. The nurse also lists every test and medicine that a patient receives while he or she is in the hospital.

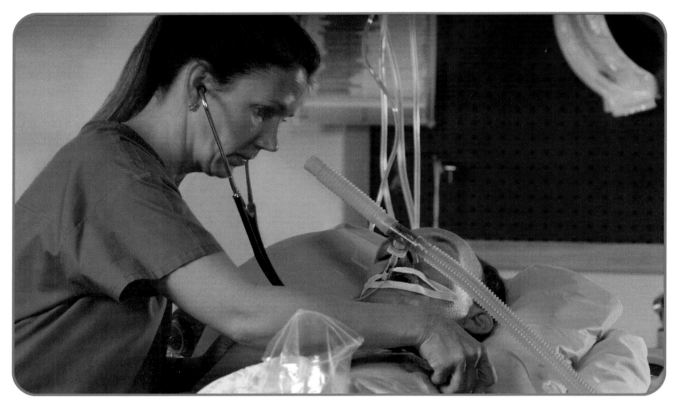

Doctors in the ER

Emergency room doctors are very busy!
They care for many patients. The doctors
examine the patients to decide on the
treatment for each one. They often order
medical tests such as **blood tests** or **x-rays**.
Medical tests help doctors learn more
about a patient's illness. Doctors may also
prescribe medicines. Medicines can be
given to patients in different ways. Some
medicines are pills that must be swallowed,
and others are given through a patient's IV.

Closing deep cuts

Many patients who visit the ER have serious cuts or scrapes. Patients with deep cuts often need **stitches**. Stitches are pieces of thread that hold cuts together so they can heal. Doctors use curved needles to stitch the cuts closed. Before they begin, doctors put medicine on the skin around the cut to **numb** it. When the skin is numb, patients do not feel any pain as their cuts are stitched together. For some cuts, doctors use **wound glue**. Wound glue is a type of glue that holds skin together so cuts can heal.

After stitching a cut, the doctor wraps bandages around the injury.

Good to go!

Patients usually stay in the emergency room for only a short time. If patients are very sick or badly injured, doctors admit them to the hospital. Patients who are admitted are moved from the ER to a different area of the hospital. Hospital workers in each area of the hospital care for patients with different types of illnesses and injuries. When patients are well again, they are **discharged**, or allowed to go home.

Special care

Some doctors are specially trained to treat certain illnesses and injuries. These doctors are called **specialists**. **Pediatricians** are specialists who treat children. They know a lot about the diseases that children often get. In many hospitals, pediatricians work in the ER in case sick or injured children need care.

Surgeons are specialists who perform **surgeries**, or operations. They are sometimes called to the ER when patients are so badly injured that they need surgery to stabilize them. A patient having surgery is moved to an **operating room**.

The surgeon on the left is talking to an ER doctor about a patient's surgery.

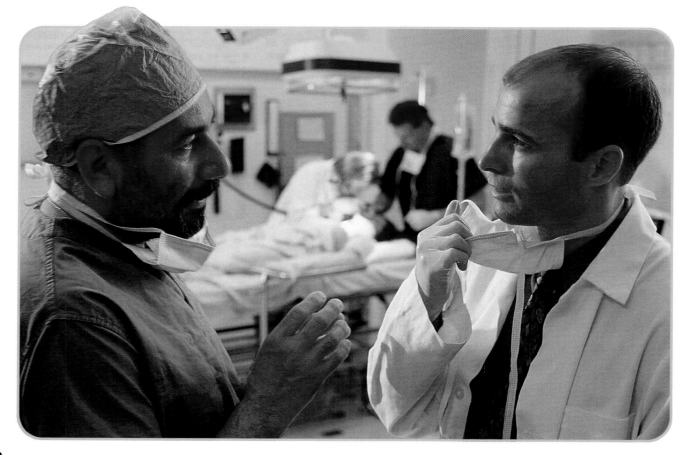

Bone specialists

Orthopedic doctors care for patients who have damaged bones or muscles. The word "ortho" means "bone." Some injuries, including broken bones, get better only if the injured part of the body is kept very still. To keep an injured arm or leg still, the doctor puts a cast on it, as shown right. It may take several weeks for a broken bone to heal.

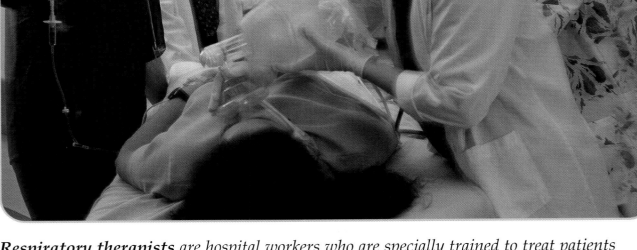

Respiratory therapists are hospital workers who are specially trained to treat patients with serious breathing problems. For example, they help people whose lungs have been hurt by breathing in smoke from a fire.

Medical tests

Doctors sometimes send their patients for medical tests to find out exactly what is wrong with them. A common medical test is a blood test. A trained **laboratory technician** called a **phlebotomist** collects blood samples from patients.

Taking blood

To collect a blood sample, the technician pricks a patient's arm with a needle. The patient's blood flows into a small tube, which is attached to the needle. The prick from the needle may hurt for a few seconds, but it is over quickly.

Each blood sample is labeled with a patient's name to make sure the test results are given to the right person.

A closer look

Blood samples are brought to a **laboratory** or "lab" for testing. A laboratory is a room in a hospital filled with equipment for doing medical tests. Lab technicians test the blood samples. They use **microscopes** to examine the samples. The results from each blood test are given to the ER doctors. The results help the doctors diagnose each patient's illness.

Lab technicians work quickly and carefully to test blood samples for ER doctors.

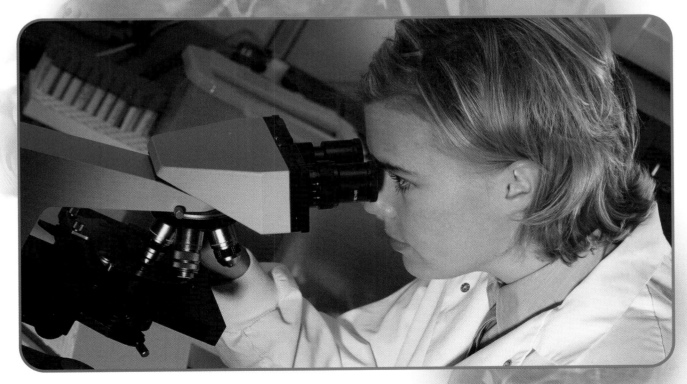

This lab technician is using a microscope to examine a blood sample. The microscope has powerful lenses that help her see the blood up close so she can check it for signs of illness.

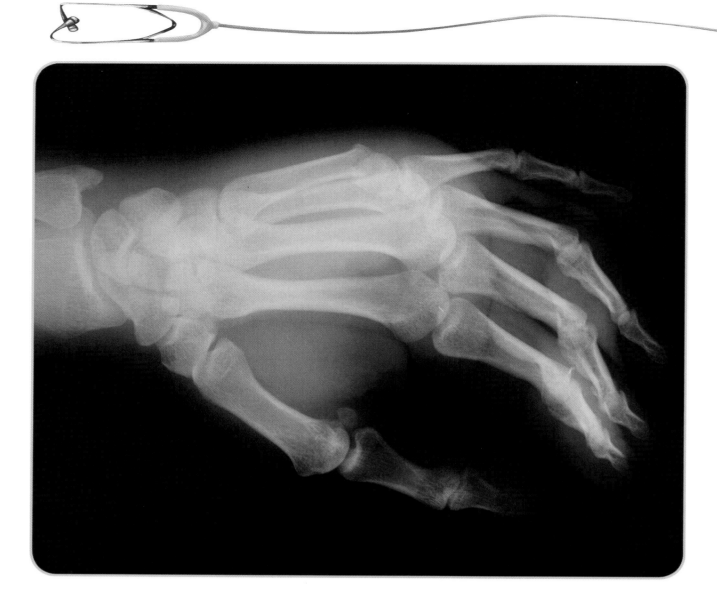

Excellent x-rays

Some ER patients have broken bones or other injuries inside their bodies. Other patients may have problems in their hearts, lungs, or other organs that doctors cannot see while examining them.

Doctors send these patients to the **radiology room** for x-rays. An x-ray is a photograph of the inside of a person's body. **Radiology technicians** are hospital workers who are trained to take x-rays.

Getting an x-ray

A radiology technician reads a patient's chart before taking an x-ray. The ER doctor makes notes on the chart to tell the technician which areas of the body need x-rays. To take an x-ray, the radiology technician often asks the patient to lie on a table. He or she then positions the patient's body for the x-rays and places a large camera over the body part the doctor needs to see. The patient must stay still while the x-rays are being taken so the pictures will not be blurry.

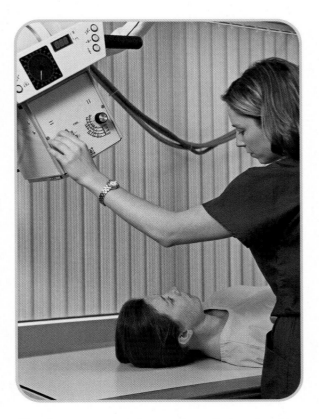

Getting x-rays takes only a few minutes and does not hurt at all.

Reading x-rays

After the x-rays are taken, a doctor called a **radiologist** examines the pictures. By looking at the x-rays, he or she can see if there is a broken bone or other injury inside the body. The radiologist then sends the results of the x-rays to the ER doctor.

Well-trained workers

Becoming a hospital worker in an emergency room takes plenty of hard work. You must learn a lot about the human body and how to care for it. To become a doctor, nurse, or other hospital worker, you must study medicine at a college or a university.

On-the-job training

In addition to learning at school, many doctors must work as **interns**. Interns are doctors who are training to become specialists. They treat patients under the **supervision**, or careful watch, of experienced specialists.

Caring people

Hospitals always need caring and hard-working people. In some communities, there are not enough doctors, nurses, or other hospital workers. The hospital workers in these communities must work long hours to treat everyone who needs medical help. Hospital workers in the ER are important community helpers. Their jobs are challenging, but they are also very rewarding!

Learning more

Learn more about doctors, nurses, and other hospital workers by visiting these great websites:

• www.kidshealth.org/kid/feel_better/

• www.nfpa.org/sparky/cool_archive/erdoctor.html

• www.knowitall.org/kidswork/hospital/realpeople/index.html

Staying safe

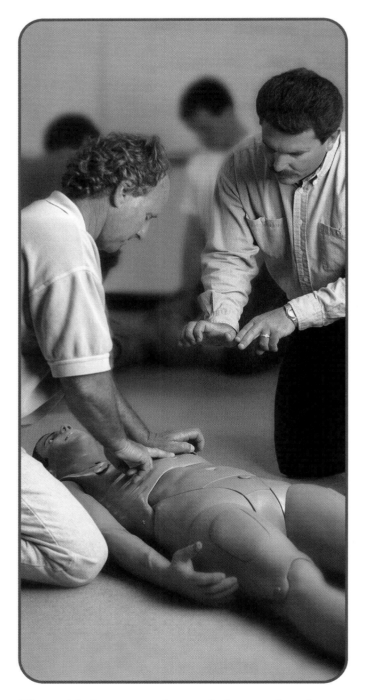

First-aid classes teach people how to bandage cuts and scrapes, what to do when someone is choking, and how to help someone who is not breathing.

Do you know how to help someone who is hurt or sick? You can learn how to help by taking a **first-aid course**. First-aid courses are available in your community. The courses will teach you how to help injured or sick people during an emergency until medical help arrives.

Call for help!

It is important for everyone to know how to get help in case of an emergency. The fastest way is by dialing 911 or another emergency-service number in your area. When you dial an emergency-service number, an **operator** will ask what kind of help you need. He or she will then send firefighters, police officers, or EMS workers to help you.

Know the rules

You can prevent emergencies by keeping yourself safe. You can stay safe by following some basic rules. Teach your family and friends these rules so that they will stay safe, too.

Safety first

Listed below are a few simple safety tips:

- Always wear a helmet while in-line skating or riding a bicycle. A helmet will protect your head if you fall. Wearing knee pads, elbow pads, and wrist guards will also help protect you.

- Always ride your bicycle on the right side of a street. You should travel in the same direction as the direction of the cars on the road. Never ride against the traffic!

- Always buckle your seatbelt when you are riding in a car.

- Learn how to swim and always follow the safety rules of the pool!

Glossary

Note: Boldfaced words that are defined in the book may not appear in the glossary.

allergic Describing a physical reaction to something such as dust, pollen, or certain foods

blood test A test done on a sample of blood

fever A body temperature that is higher than 98.6°F (37°C)

laboratory technician A person who is trained to work in a laboratory

lungs Organs inside a person's body that are used for breathing

meningitis An illness that causes a person's brain to swell

operating room A room in a hospital where operations are performed

operator A person who answers telephone calls

oxygen A gas in the air that living things breathe

pneumonia A disease that affects the lungs and can make it difficult for a person to breathe

Severe Acute Respiratory Syndrome A highly contagious disease that causes severe breathing difficulties

vein A blood vessel that carries blood to the heart

x-ray A photograph of the inside of a person's body

Index

1 2 3 4 5 6 7 8 9 0 Printed in the U.S.A. 4 3 2 1 0 9 8 7 6 5